Peabody Public Library
Columbia City, IN

J 979.7 JACKSON
Jackson, Tom,
The Columbia River / by Tom
Jackson.

SEP 25 '07

W9-AZH-016

The **Columbia** River

by Tom Jackson

Peabody Public Library
Columbia City, IN

Gareth Stevens Publishing
A WORLD ALMANAC EDUCATION GROUP COMPANY

Please visit our web site at: www.garethstevens.com
For a free color catalog describing Gareth Stevens Publishing's list of high-quality books and multimedia programs, call 1-800-542-2595 (USA) or 1-800-387-3178 (Canada). Gareth Stevens Publishing's fax: (414) 332-3567.

Library of Congress Cataloging-in-Publication Data

Jackson, Tom, 1953–
    The Columbia River / by Tom Jackson.
       p. cm. — (Rivers of North America)
    Includes bibliographical references and index.
    Contents: The electric river—From source to mouth—The life of the river—Following the trail—Nature's might—Places to visit—How rivers form.
    ISBN 0-8368-3754-1 (lib. bdg.)
    1. Columbia River—Juvenile literature. [1. Columbia River.] I. Title. II. Series.
F853.J33   2003
979.7—dc21   2003042738

This North American edition first published in 2004 by
Gareth Stevens Publishing
A World Almanac Education Group Company
330 West Olive Street, Suite 100
Milwaukee, Wisconsin 53212 USA

Original copyright © 2004 The Brown Reference Group plc. This U.S. edition copyright © 2004 by Gareth Stevens, Inc.

Author: Tom Jackson
Editor: Tom Jackson
Consultant: Judy Wheatley Maben, Education Director, Water Education Foundation
Designer: Steve Wilson
Cartographer: Mark Walker
Picture Researcher: Clare Newman
Indexer: Kay Ollerenshaw
Managing Editor: Bridget Giles
Art Director: Dave Goodman

Gareth Stevens Editor: Betsy Rasmussen
Gareth Stevens Designer: Melissa Valuch

Picture Credits: Cover: Fort Clatsop, Oregon, near the mouth of the Columbia River. (Skyscan: Jim Wark) Contents: Portland, Oregon.

Key: l–left, r–right, t–top, b–bottom.
Ardea: Ken Lucas 11t; Corbis: 14, 19; Bettmann 4t; Carol Cohen 12/13; Philip James Corwin 25r; Michael S. Lewis 15; Roger Ressmeyer 28; Bob Rowan/Progressive Image 22; Michael T. Sedam 27; Scott T. Smith 10; Getty Images: 17, 18, 20/21, 21r; Steve Satushek 6; Art Wolfe 12l; PhotoDisc: Alan & Sandy Carey 11b, 13b; D. Falconer/PhotoLink 4/5, 29t; Bruce Heinemann 26; J. Luke/PhotoLink 5t; Still Pictures: Peter Arnold/Alan Majchrowicz 8l, 8/9; U.S. Army Corps of Engineers: Wayne Buchanan 16; Bob Heims 9r, 23t, 23b, 24/25, 29b

All rights reserved. No part of this book may be reproduced, stored in a retrieval system, or transmitted in any form or by any means electronic, mechanical, photocopying, recording, or otherwise, without the prior written permission of the copyright holder.

Printed in the United States of America

1 2 3 4 5 6 7 8 9 07 06 05 04 03

Table of Contents

The Electric River

The Columbia River powers the Pacific Northwest. On its way through spectacular landscape, the river is tapped by a series of huge dams that supply electricity and water to the entire region.

The Columbia River begins in the Rocky Mountains in southern Canada and flows south, through Washington state. It then forms the northern border of Oregon, before it reaches the Pacific Ocean, over one thousand miles from its source.

Power Plants

At several places along its length, the Columbia cuts through steep gorges and canyons. The river has changed course many times, leaving dry canyons, or coulees, behind. Today, most of the river's canyons and coulees are dammed. In fact, the river is the most heavily dammed stretch of water in the world. The dams have power plants inside them that are driven by the river's current to produce electricity. The electricity made by the dams is used in factories and cities from California to Canada. Since the

Left: *Grand Coulee Dam, Washington, the largest dam on the Columbia River and in the United States. The dam has flooded a vast dry canyon, called the Grand Coulee.*

dams were built, the region has become an important industrial area, with factories that build everything from airplanes to computer chips.

Many Changes

Native groups were living beside the Columbia River more than ten thousand years ago. Non-Native people began settling in the area in the early nineteenth century. In those days, the Columbia was a wild, rugged river, which tumbled over many waterfalls and rapids. The fast-running water was filled with millions of salmon and many other types of wildlife.

Today, however, the river's water collects behind huge dams, and most stretches of the river are now much deeper than they once were. The deep water covers the rapids and waterfalls, forming long, artificial lakes. The changes to the river's natural landscape have had a negative effect on wildlife, especially the salmon population.

Left: *The Columbia River Gorge on the border of Washington and Oregon. Before dams tamed the river, the gorge was filled with waterfalls and rapids.*

Below: *Downtown Portland, Oregon, the largest city and main port on the Columbia.*

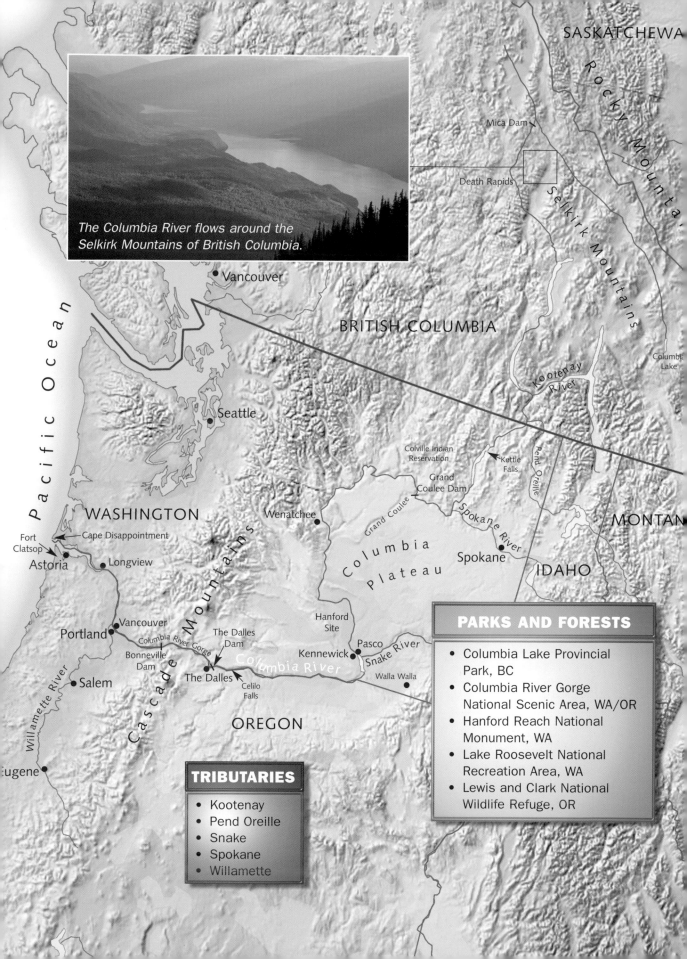

SASKATCHEWA

Rocky Mountain

Mica Dam

Death Rapids

Selkirk Mountains

Columbia Lake

The Columbia River flows around the Selkirk Mountains of British Columbia.

Pacific Ocean

Vancouver

BRITISH COLUMBIA

Kootenay River

Seattle

Colville Indian Reservation

Kettle Falls

Grand Coulee Dam

Pend Oreille

MONTAN

WASHINGTON

Wenatchee

Grand Coulee

Columbia Plateau

Spokane River

Spokane

Fort Clatsop

Cape Disappointment

Astoria

Longview

Cascade Mountains

Hanford Site

Pasco

Kennewick

Snake River

Walla Walla

IDAHO

Portland

Vancouver

Columbia River Gorge

The Dalles Dam

Bonneville Dam

Columbia River

Willamette River

Salem

The Dalles

Celilo Falls

Eugene

OREGON

TRIBUTARIES

- Kootenay
- Pend Oreille
- Snake
- Spokane
- Willamette

PARKS AND FORESTS

- Columbia Lake Provincial Park, BC
- Columbia River Gorge National Scenic Area, WA/OR
- Hanford Reach National Monument, WA
- Lake Roosevelt National Recreation Area, WA
- Lewis and Clark National Wildlife Refuge, OR

From Source to Mouth

The waters of the mighty Columbia River have transformed the landscape, cutting canyons, coulees, and gorges as the river flows from the Rockies of Canada to the Pacific coast of Oregon.

The Columbia River is the second-largest river flowing to the west coast of North America. Only the Yukon River in Canada and Alaska carries more water to the Pacific. The Columbia is 1,243 miles (2,000 kilometers) long and collects water from 259,000 square miles (670,000 sq km). Although the Columbia only flows through two U.S. states, it gathers water from smaller rivers flowing through Idaho, Montana, Nevada, Wyoming, and Utah.

Northern Route

The river's source is Columbia Lake, which lies in a high valley between two mountain ranges— the Canadian Rockies to the east and the Selkirk range to the west. The lake is almost one-half mile (0.8 meters) above sea level. Melting snow from the peaks above feed the river, which flows north for its first 200 miles (320 km).

KEY FACTS	
Length:	1,243 miles (2,000 km)
Drainage basin:	259,000 square miles (670,000 sq km)
Source:	Columbia Lake, British Columbia
Mouth:	Cape Disappointment, Washington
Natural features:	Death Rapids, Grand Coulee, Celilo Falls, Columbia River Gorge
Economic uses:	Hydroelectricity, irrigation, water for cities, fishing, recreation
Major dams:	Mica, Grand Coulee, The Dalles, Bonneville
Major cities:	The Dalles, Portland, and Astoria, Oregon; Vancouver and Longview, Washington

The river then makes a U-turn around the Selkirk Mountains and heads south toward the U.S. and Canada border. About 50 miles (80 km) downstream from this bend, the water runs through Death Rapids, once a dangerous stretch of fast-running water that claimed the lives of many canoeists. Like many of the rapids and waterfalls on the Columbia River, the mighty Death Rapids have been tamed by a dam.

Continuing its journey south, the Columbia is met by the Kootenay River before it flows into the state of Washington. The river continues flowing through mountains until it is met by the Spokane River, about 60 miles (97 km) south of the U.S. and Canada border. Here, the Columbia swings to the west and flows across the Columbia Plateau.

Through Lava

The Columbia Plateau is a vast area of lava that covers most of central Washington, spreading into Idaho and Oregon. It was formed millions of years ago when lava flowed out of cracks in the ground and spread out over the land. The lava then cooled to form the plateau.

The river itself has made many changes to the plateau, by creating coulees and scablands. Coulees are dry canyons that were formed during ice ages many thousands of years ago. During the ice ages, the river was often blocked by sheets of ice. Every so often, the river would break through the ice and rush in streams over the plateau. The streams carried blocks of ice and rock, which cut through the softer sections of lava making coulees. Over

Below: *A view of Grand Coulee, a dry canyon in Washington. Most of the coulee is now a reservoir.*

Left: *Several small streams tumblc down the side of the Columbia River Gorge, forming many spectacular waterfalls, such as this one on the Oregon side.*

Right: *The Columbia River flows past Astoria before meeting the ocean a few miles beyond.*

the years, the river changed course several times. As it changed direction, the river left the coulees to dry out. (Today, many coulees have been filled with river water again and are used as reservoirs.) The river only washed away the softest parts of the plateau. Patches of harder rock remain on the surface, forming bare hills named "scabs."

Mighty Gorge

The Columbia then flows south, skirting the scab-lands, until it reaches Pasco near the Oregon border. Here it is met by its largest tributary, the Snake River.

After meeting the Snake, the Columbia makes another change of direction, flowing west toward the ocean and forming the border between Washington and Oregon. Beyond the city of The Dalles, the river enters the Columbia River Gorge. The gorge cuts through the Cascade Mountains and is 4,000 feet (1,220 m) deep at some points and over 80 miles (130 km) long. The gorge used to be filled with rapids and waterfalls, but today the dammed water runs in a calm, deep channel.

Beyond the gorge, the river flows past Portland, Oregon. The Willamette River, another important tributary, joins the flow here. The Columbia then flows into a large natural harbor at Astoria, Oregon, where the river's mouth is about 6 miles (10 km) across. The Columbia finally empties into the Pacific Ocean at Cape Disappointment.

2 The Life of the River

The Columbia River was once famous for its salmon, but today, people also enjoy the wealth of wildlife living in the river's wet forests and on the cold, desertlike scablands.

The weather in the Columbia River Basin is not as cold as some places that are that far north. This is because the area is warmed by winds that blow in from the Pacific Ocean. The mountains that surround the basin also have a major effect on the weather in the region, creating a range of different types of habitat—from desert to forest—along the river.

Rain Shadow
The air coming in from the ocean carries a lot of moisture with it. Most

Above:
Sagebrush grows all around barren scabs of hard rock on the open plateau of Oregon.

10

WHITE STURGEONS

White sturgeons (right) live in the Columbia River, although they are rare. These giant fish are the largest river fish in North America. Most are 12 feet (3.6 m) long, while a few grow to 20 feet (6 meters) and weigh more than 1,000 pounds (454 kilograms). Their bodies are covered with rows of bony plates, and they have a long snout with thick, sucking lips. Like salmon, white sturgeons swim from the ocean to small streams to breed.

of this falls as rain on the Cascade Mountains, which run north to south near the coast. The mountains surrounding the Columbia River Gorge get about 60 inches (150 cm) of rain every year. With all this rain, forests of fir and pine trees grow on the slopes.

Once the wind has passed over the Cascades, it is much drier. When it gets to the scablands of the Columbia Plateau, the air

has very little moisture left. The plateau gets only about 6 inches (15 cm) of rain every year. This is called the rain shadow effect—the mountains block rain from getting to the land beyond.

With so little rain, the Columbia Plateau is almost a desert, and very few trees manage to survive there. Sagebrush is the largest plant growing in the area. This woody plant grows into bushes up to 12 feet (3.5 m)

Below: *River otters feed on small river animals, such as crabs, snails, and small fish.*

Above: *A sockeye salmon attempts to leap over a waterfall on its way upriver to breed. The fish rest beneath falls to gather their strength for the next push upstream.*

Above right: *A lush forest above the Columbia River Gorge with a stepped trail for tourists.*

tall. Sagebrush has small leaves covered in tiny hairs, which help the plants retain water. Prickly pears and tough grasses also grow on the scablands.

The mountains around the northern stretch of the river receive more rain and snow than the plateau, and spruce, hemlock, and fir trees grow on the slopes. Many wildflowers, such as yellow arum and dogwood, also grow in the forests.

Highs and Lows

The animals that live on the river's mountains are different from those on the Columbia Plateau. Black-

tailed deer and bighorn sheep are common in the Cascade Mountains, while moose and grizzly bears are common in British Columbia. Bald eagles and vesper sparrows are birds often seen in the river's highlands.

Bobcats, coyotes, and elk are the largest animals living among the shrubs of the plateau. Pheasants and sage grouse live on the plateau all year-round.

Water birds, such as geese and ducks, migrate through the Columbia area each year, and millions of them break their journey at the river's wetlands, including

the artificial lakes along the Columbia's route. Mink, beavers, and river otters are a few animals that live all along the banks of the Columbia and its many tributaries.

Disappearing Fish

More than six hundred species of fish live in the Columbia River, including perch, steelhead trout, lamprey, smelt, and five types of salmon—chinook, sockeye, chum, coho, and pink. Salmon spend most of their lives at sea but swim up the river to breed in the fast-running streams near the river's source. The fish are strong swimmers and can leap through rapids and over waterfalls to get to their spawning area.

Before dams were built across the Columbia in the twentieth century, the river had more salmon in it than any other river in North America. Today, only a fraction remain because the fish cannot swim past the huge dams to get to their breeding grounds. Dam-builders have developed ways to allow the fish to get past some of the Columbia's dams. With this help, the numbers of salmon in the river are beginning to rise again.

HOWLS IN THE FOREST

As night falls over the Columbia River, eerie howls fill the air, sweeping through the forested slopes of British Columbia. These ghostly noises are made by a gray wolf (below) calling across the valley. Wolves live in family groups called packs. Gray wolves, also called timber wolves, live out in the open. Wolfs generally hunt together, chasing prey. Wolves can smell their prey from more than one mile (1.6 km) away. Gray wolves used to live in most parts of the Columbia Basin, but most have been overhunted by people. Although wolves never attack humans, many people think they are dangerous. Only a few wolf packs remain in the Columbia River Basin, mainly in British Columbia. They are shy and keep out of the way of people.

3 Following the Trail

The Columbia River region was not settled by non-Native people until 150 years ago. After years of exploration, thousands came to the area following the now-famous Oregon Trail.

People have lived beside the Columbia River for at least ten thousand years. When Europeans explored the river in the late eighteenth century, there were several Native groups living in the area. The groups living near the mouth of the river had a different way of life from the people who lived east of the Cascade Mountains on the open scablands of the Columbia Plateau.

Village Communities

Most people living on the lower Columbia were Chinooks. Chinooks lived in large communities along the Willamette River and beside the Columbia close to where Portland stands today. The Chinooks and other nearby groups, such as the Clakama, Kalapuya, Multnomah, and Tillamook, lived in longhouses. Villages had several longhouses,

Below: *Inside a Chinook lodge. The people in this picture have sloping heads because it was a Chinook custom to deform the skulls of newborn babies with hard boards placed in cradles.*

PIT HOUSES OF THE PLATEAU

Archaeologists have found the remains of the pit-house villages built by the Spokane, Cayuse, and the other Native people who lived beside the upper section of the Columbia River. A pit house was built over a round pit dug about 6 feet (1.8 m) into the ground. The walls were made of posts, which supported a cone-shaped roof.

The roof was covered in bark and earth. The front door of most pit houses was a hole at the top of the roof, which also served as a smokehole. People climbed in and out using a ladder made from a log with foot holes cut into it. The largest pit houses were 60 feet wide (18 m) wide, but most were about half this size.

each with room for two or three large families. Chinooks gathered fruits, roots, and nuts and fished for salmon in the river. One species of salmon in the Columbia is named for the Chinook people.

Strict Society

Chinook society had three ranks or classes. The chiefs and their wealthy relatives belonged to the upper class. The common people had fewer possessions than the upper class and formed the middle class. Most Chinooks belonged to this group.

Slaves were the lowest ranking group. They actually belonged to higher-ranking Chinooks and could not own any property. Slaves were captured during raids on neighboring groups. The Chinooks were traders, and they traded their slaves along with other products.

Chinook chiefs often held

Above: *The remains of a pit house in British Columbia. The pit has been filled in but parts of the roof remain.*

Above: *Native fishers use nets on long poles to catch salmon at Celilo Falls in 1956, before dammed water swamped the falls.*

a feast, called a potlatch, to show off their high rank and wealth. Potlatches lasted for several days. The chief fed his guests and gave away many of his valuable things. Rival chiefs competed with each other during potlatches by destroying many of their valuable items, such as copper shields.

People of the Plateau

The Native groups living in the scablands and mountains of the upper section of the Columbia River did not have the

same kind of society. Cayuse, Colville, Nez Perce, and Spokane people lived in this region. They lived in small bands made up of a single family. Each band controlled an area of land, and they were not supposed to gather food from another band's territory.

During the summer, these bands traveled around their territory collecting food. The plateau peoples ate wild fruits and roots and caught salmon from the Columbia River. At the height of the breeding season, the river was filled with fish. The fish were plentiful beneath rapids and waterfalls, as they tried to leap upstream through the fast-running waters. Two of the best fishing locations used by the Natives were Kettle Falls in northeast Washington and Celilo Falls, which used to be a few miles (km) upstream from where The Dalles Dam now stands on the Washington and Oregon border. European explorers described seeing thousands of Native people catching salmon at these places.

While on the move, the bands slept in simple shelters covered with woven mats or sagebrush branches. When winter arrived, the bands built shelters called pit houses. These were deep, round pits covered with cone-shaped roofs of wood and earth.

Explorers Arrive

The first maps of the Columbia River were made by Spanish explorer Martin de Auguilar in the early seventeenth century. He labeled the Columbia as the River of the West.

At the time, European explorers were looking for the Northwest Passage —a water route between China and Europe that went around or through North America, joining the Atlantic and Pacific Oceans. De Auguilar thought that the Columbia just might be a way through.

Below: *U.S. explorers Meriwether Lewis and William Clark examine their surroundings after reaching the mouth of the Columbia River in 1805.*

In 1765, British soldier Major Robert Rogers named the river the Ouragan (later spelled Oregon), which is French for hurricane and sounded similar to the name used by Native people. The region around the river was later named the Oregon Territory. This territory is now covered by Oregon, Washington, and parts of Idaho, Wyoming, and British Columbia.

Two Claims

The first non-Natives to travel up the Columbia were led by U.S. explorer Robert Gray. In 1792, he sailed into the mouth of the river, which he renamed the Columbia for his ship. After Gray's voyage, the United States claimed the Oregon Territory. However, just a few weeks later, William Broughton, a British naval officer, sailed even further up the river, past where the city of Portland now stands. He made a detailed map of the river and claimed the region for his own country.

Lewis and Clark

In 1805, U.S. explorers Meriwether Lewis and William Clark traveled from St. Louis, Missouri,

THE CAYUSE WAR

The settlement of the Oregon Territory by pioneers was not always peaceful. One of the bloodiest events was the Cayuse War (1847–1848). The Cayuse people lived near where the Columbia River is joined by the Snake River in southern Washington. The first pioneers to settle in this area were led by Marcus Whitman, a doctor originally from New York. Whitman and his friends had arrived in 1836 and lived peacefully with the Cayuse until 1847.

In that year, some new settlers came to live with Whitman. A few were suffering from measles when they arrived, and the disease spread to the Cayuse. Because the Native people had not previously been exposed to the disease, many of their children died or were brain damaged. The Cayuse thought Whitman had poisoned their children, and they killed him (left) and twelve other settlers. The U.S. Army was sent to protect the settlers, and over the next year, the soldiers killed nearly all of the Cayuse people.

Above: The trading post at Astoria, Oregon, in the 1840s, with the wide Columbia River beyond.

to the Snake River in Idaho. They followed the Snake and then the Columbia to its mouth, where they built Fort Clatsop near to where the port of Astoria, Oregon, is today.

In the years following this famous journey, settlers began to arrive in the Oregon Territory. In 1834, the first pioneers arrived in the area. They had taken the Oregon Trail—a long overland route west from Missouri to the Pacific Ocean—a route similar to the one taken by Lewis and Clark. In 1843, another nine hundred settlers arrived. From then on, hundreds of Americans traveled the Oregon Trail every year.

During this time, the Oregon Territory was shared by the United States and Britain. In 1846, they agreed to divide the territory. Britain got the northern part, which is now included in British Columbia, Canada, and the United States took control of the southern area.

Building Cities

The dry scablands around the upper Columbia did not attract very many settlers.

Most headed west of the Cascade Mountains to live along the southern stretch of the river. The river's first towns—Astoria, Vancouver, and Portland—were built here, and they are still the river's main urban centers.

Astoria was founded in 1811 by the wealthy U.S. fur trader John Jacob Astor. It was the first U.S. settlement to be built west of the Rockies. In 1825, the British government built Fort Vancouver, a trading post on the north side of the river. French-Canadian trappers built their cabins across the river from Vancouver, where the Willamette River joins the flow and where Portland stands today.

In 1845, Portland was founded by Asa Lovejoy and Francis Pettygrove, two settlers from New England. The settlement grew fast and was soon the largest city on the Columbia River. The people of Portland made a living working in the lumber, wool, and salmon industries. By the late 1880s, there were more than forty canneries along the river, packing salmon that would be sold to people around the world.

Below: *Fishers haul in a catch of salmon at the end of the nineteenth century. Today, there are far fewer salmon in the Columbia.*

In 1905, Portland held a world's fair, attracting people to the city. That year, three million people visited and many of them stayed.

During the 1930s, Portland and the Columbia River began to change. The lumber mills were forced to close when huge fires destroyed forests in the area. At the same time, however, the first big dams were being built. The dams not only supplied cheap electricity for factories, but the water they collected was used to irrigate crops on new farms across the region.

THE TILLAMOOK BURN

In 1933, a fire wiped out 375 square miles (971 sq km) of mountain forest (below) near Tillamook, Oregon, southwest of Portland. The wood from the destroyed trees would have been enough to build one million five-bedroom houses. Many of the sawmills in Portland were forced to close after the fire, which was named the Tillamook Burn. After several more large fires, a new forest was planted in 1949. Today, the hills around Tillamook are thickly forested again, and the area's lumber industry has now recovered.

4 Nature's Might

The power of the mighty Columbia has been harnessed by the river's many dams. Throughout the Pacific Northwest, cities, factories, and farms have benefited from the river's resources.

The Columbia River is the most heavily dammed waterway in the world. There are fourteen large dams on the Columbia itself, and even more on the river's large tributaries, such as the Snake and Spokane Rivers.

Damming has caused enormous change in the landscape and wildlife of the area. For example, there are now more than 250 artificial lakes in the river basin, and one important industry—salmon fishing—has been badly damaged. The dams produce electricity, collect water for irrigating crops, and tame the river for cargo ships to travel inland.

Above: *A sprinkler system sprays water from the Columbia River onto potato fields in Washington.*

SAVING THE COLUMBIA'S SALMON

The Columbia River was once famous for its salmon. In the 1880s, the river contained more than sixteen million salmon—more than any other river in North America. The fish were caught in nets and canned in riverside plants. The canaries packed 30 million pounds (13 million kg) of salmon every year.

Adult salmon live in the ocean and swim up rivers to spawn (breed). The adults die after breeding. The salmon eggs hatch and smolts, young fish (below), spend a short time feeding on the river bed. Then they swim down the river and out to sea.

When dams were built across the river, the salmon could not get to their spawning grounds, and their numbers began to decrease. Dambuilders constructed fish ladders (above right) so salmon could climb over dams. A fish ladder is a concrete channel with a series of steps. Water flows

down the channel creating artificial rapids, and salmon jump from step to step. Ladders have been built at four dams on the Columbia.

Some salmon manage to climb over the dams and breed with each other, but their problems are not over. As young salmon make their way to the sea, many are sucked into the dams' power plants and killed by the giant spinning turbines. At some places, young fish are collected in tanks and carried around the dam in trucks or on barges. Other dams have screens in front of their turbines, which guide the young fish into safe channels through the dam. These measures seem to be helping, and in the last few years, the number of salmon has been rising slowly.

Because of this, the region's economy has been boosted by the dams.

Taming the River
Before dams were built on the river, the Columbia had many rapids and waterfalls that stopped boats from traveling upriver. In 1896, a canal was dug around the Cascade Rapids east of Portland. A few years later, a similar system allowed ships to travel past the rapids near The Dalles, Oregon, a few miles upriver.

These early projects were very small compared to the dams built during the twentieth century. In the early 1930s, the United

States was gripped by the Great Depression. Millions of people did not have jobs and traveled across the country looking for work. Franklin D. Roosevelt, the U.S. president at the time, started a massive building program across the United States to create jobs and boost the nation's economy. The president's plan was called the "New Deal" and provided the money to build the Bonneville and Grand Coulee Dams, the first giant dams on the Columbia.

The Bonneville Dam, 40 miles (64 km) to the east of Portland, took four years to build and was completed in 1937. In 1941, Grand Coulee Dam, the largest dam in the United States, was built farther upstream on the rugged Columbia Plateau.

Over the next thirty years many more dams were built on the Columbia. The last to be constructed was British Columbia's Mica Dam, which was completed in 1973.

River Uses

All the dams have power plants attached to them, which turn the energy of the river water flowing through them into electricity. Making electricity in this way is much less expensive than burning fuel. This supply of cheap electricity helped the

United States during World War II (1939–1945). It was used by aluminum plants, aircraft factories, and shipyards. Radioactive plutonium used in the first nuclear bombs was made in a plant at Hanford in Washington. The plant was powered by the dams.

After the war, companies came to the area to make the most of the cheap electricity. Today, cities such as Seattle and Portland are home to large companies, including aircraft-manufacturer Boeing and Nike, the sports shoe giant.

Above: *Large containerships sailing up the Columbia from the ocean to the port at Portland.*

ROSE FESTIVAL

The city of Portland has been famous for its roses since the nineteenth century, when gardeners in the city realized that the area's weather was good for growing these beautiful flowers. Every year since 1907, the people of Portland have celebrated their roses with the Portland Rose Festival. Today, almost two million people visit the festival, traveling thousands of miles to the month-long event. The festival earns the city more than eighty million dollars each year. The festival highlights include an airshow, car races, the Grand Floral Parade of horse riders, marching bands, and floats decorated with flowers. The festival's fairground is beside the Willamette River.

Right: *Visitors enjoy the carnival atmosphere of the Portland Rose Festival.*

Above: *An orchard growing beside the Columbia River. The land is watered by the river, while the dry, unirrigated plateau can be seen beyond.*

Water Control

The river's dams have raised the level of the water so much that most of the river no longer has any rapids or waterfalls. Large barges can pass through locks in the dams and can now travel from the port of Astoria, at the river's mouth, to Lewiston, Idaho, by way of the Snake River. The river between Portland and the Pacific Ocean has been deepened so that oceangoing ships can reach the city's port, which is nearly 100 miles (160 km) from the coast. The boats on the river carry crops, such as wheat from northern Oregon, wood chips, and lumber.

East of the Cascade Mountains, the river flows through the dry lands of the Columbia Plateau. Before the dams were built, most of the plateau's land was too dry to grow crops. A few farmers did manage to make a living in the region, however. At the end of the nineteenth century, apple and pear orchards were planted near Wenatchee, Washington, and beside the Hood River in northern Oregon. Water for them was channeled from other rivers.

Today, water from the Columbia's reservoirs has turned the dry plateau into green farmland. Most of the irrigated farms grow wheat and fruits, such as cherries, plums, and apricots. The area is also one of the world's main producers of seeds and flower bulbs. Farms sell seeds for mint and grass plants and produce iris, tulip, and daffodil bulbs.

GRAND COULEE DAM

Grand Coulee Dam (below) is the largest single piece of concrete in the United States. The dam is 5,233 feet (1,595 m) long and as tall as a forty-six-story building. The reservoir behind the dam forms a lake that snakes 151 miles (243 km) along the river valley all the way into Canada. The water in the lake is 350 feet (106 m) higher than the original river. Tourists visit the lake to hike, camp, and fish. Salmon cannot get past the giant dam into the lake, and fishers mainly hook walleye, which were introduced to the lake in the 1960s.

The huge dam also pushes water into Grand Coulee—a 27-mile- (43-km-) long canyon formed by the Columbia River a few million years ago. The river has since changed course, and the water stored in Grand Coulee is used to irrigate farms on the dry scablands of the Columbia Plateau.

5 Places to Visit

The Columbia River is known for both the beauty of its natural features and its enormous artificial structures. Tourists also visit the many historic sites that are preserved in the region.

❶ Fairmont Hot Springs, BC

A resort with three natural springs that flow from deep inside the Rocky Mountains close to Columbia Lake. Over 1 million gallons (3.8 million liters) of water flow over falls and into pools around the town every day.

❷ Franklin D. Roosevelt Lake, WA

This lake was created in 1941, when Grand Coulee Dam was completed. The lake was named for the U.S. president at the time. It is now the center of the Franklin D. Roosevelt National Recreation Area. Visitors enjoy boating, fishing, and swimming. Historic sites such as Fort Spokane and St. Paul's Mission are also in the park.

❸ Chief Joseph Memorial, WA

A memorial to the Nez Perce chief who led a band of Native fighters in a war against the U.S. Army in 1877. He refused to move from his homeland in Oregon and attacked settlers in the area. After a prolonged chase across the region, Chief Joseph surrendered and went to live beside the Columbia River in Washington.

❹ Crown Point Overlook, WA

This viewpoint close to the highway gives breathtaking views of the Grand Coulee Dam and its surrounding countryside. In the summer, the history of the Columbia River is told in a laser show at the dam. The lasers

28

create images on the dam's huge concrete wall and spillway. People watching from the overlook can listen to the story on the radio.

⑤ Hanford Site, WA

In 1943, the DuPont Company built a plant here to make plutonium metal for the nuclear bombs used in World War II (1939–1945). After the war, the nuclear plant was converted to produce electricity.

Hanford Site, one of the first nuclear plants in the world.

⑥ Columbia River Gorge

The Columbia River Gorge is a popular destination for tourists, who come to hike along wilderness trails and admire the scenery. In the last twenty years, the gorge has become a major windsurfing spot. People come from all over the world to ride the strong winds that whistle through the spectacular canyon.

Windsurfers ride the wind through the Columbia River Gorge.

⑦ Bonneville Dam

This dam was named for Benjamin Bonneville, a U.S. Army captain, who explored the whole region. It is the second-largest dam in the Columbia River Basin, after Grand Coulee. The dam has a large lock in it that allows seagoing ships to travel into the reservoir behind. By using this lock and others like it in smaller dams upstream, ships can travel from the ocean all the way to Lewiston, Idaho.

8 Mount St. Helens, WA

Mount St. Helens is a volcano about 40 miles (64 km) north of the Columbia River. In 1980, Mount St. Helens erupted violently, killing fifty-seven people. The eruption blasted away more than 1,000 feet (300 m) from the mountain's peak and created a huge crater (below). The force from the explosion flattened millions of trees. The heat melted snow on the mountain, causing floods and mudslides. A huge area was covered in a layer of ash.

⑨ Sauvie Island, OR

Before it meets the Columbia just west of Portland, the Willamette River splits into two channels. The land between these two channels is Sauvie Island, one of the largest river islands in North America. Sauvie Island has many farms, but its central area is a wildlife reserve.

⑩ Cape Disappointment

This high headland on the north side of the mouth of the Columbia River was named by Captain John Meares in 1788, when he realized that the river did not connect the Pacific Ocean with the Atlantic. A lighthouse, built 150 years ago, still operates as a warning to ships coming in and out the Columbia River.

How Rivers Form

Rivers have many features that are constantly changing in shape. The illustration below shows how these features are created.

Rivers flow from mountains to oceans, receiving water from rain, melting snow, and underground springs. Rivers collect their water from an area called the river basin. High mountain ridges form the divides between river basins.

Tributaries join the main river at places called confluences. Rivers flow down steep mountain slopes quickly but slow as they near the ocean and gather more water. Slow rivers have many meanders (wide turns) and often change course.

Near the mouth, levees (piles of mud) build up on the banks. The levees stop water from draining into the river, creating areas of swamp.

❶ Glacier: An ice mass that melts into river water.

❷ Lake: The source of many rivers; may be fed by springs or precipitation.

❸ Rapids: Shallow water that flows quickly.

❹ Waterfall: Formed when a river wears away softer rock, making a step in the riverbed.

❺ Canyon: Formed when a river cuts a channel through rock.

❻ Floodplain: A place where rivers often flood flat areas, depositing mud.

❼ Oxbow lake: River bend cut off when a river changes course, leaving water behind.

❽ Estuary: River mouth where river and ocean water mix together.

❾ Delta: Triangular river mouth created when mud islands form, splitting the flow into several channels called distributaries.

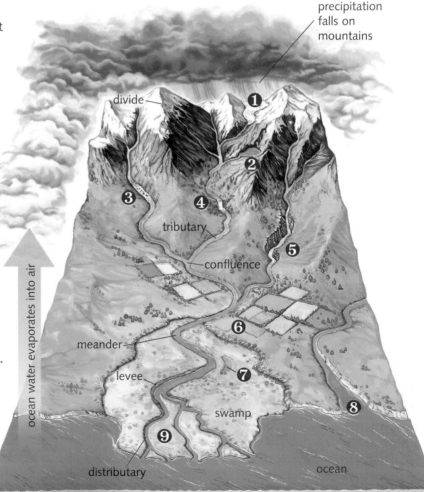

precipitation falls on mountains

divide

tributary

confluence

ocean water evaporates into air

meander

levee

swamp

distributary

ocean

Glossary

basin The area drained by a river and its tributaries.

canal A manmade waterway used for navigation or irrigation.

confluence The place where rivers meet.

dam A constructed barrier across a river that controls the flow of water.

gorge A narrow, steep-sided valley or canyon.

habitat The place where animals and plants naturally live.

hydroelectricity Electricity made by generators driven by flowing water.

irrigation Watering crops with water from a river, lake, or other source.

lock A section of a river that is enclosed by gates. The level of water inside the lock can be raised or lowered so boats can travel between stretches of water that are at different levels.

rapids Shallow parts of a river where the water runs very fast.

reservation An area of land set aside for a particular purpose. Many Native groups have reservations on which they can live.

skull Head bone that contains the brain.

source The place where a river begins.

spawning ground An area of water where fish, such as salmon, gather to breed.

tributary A river that flows into a larger river at a confluence.

valley A hollow channel cut by a river, usually between ranges of hills or mountains.

waterway A river or canal that boats can travel on.

For Further Information

Books

Hirschi, Ron. *Salmon.* Carolrhoda Books, 2000.

Katschke, Judy. *Snake River.* Raintree/Steck-Vaughn, 1998.

Layman, William D. *Native River: The Columbia Remembered.* Washington State University Press, 2002.

Rapp, Valerie. *Life in a River.* Lerner Publications, 2003.

Web Sites

Grand Coulee Dam
www.grandcouleedam.com

The Power of the Columbia
www.bpa.gov/Power/pl/columbia/index.html

Virtual World Columbia River
www.nationalgeographic.com/earthpulse/columbia/index_flash.html

Index

Peabody Public Library
Columbia City, IN

Peabody Public Library
Columbia City, IN